REPETITIONS & MISADVENTURES OF IMMORTALS

REPETITIONS & MISADVENTURES OF IMMORTALS

Paul Éluard & Max Ernst

Translated by Gian Lombardo

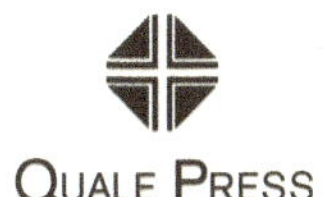

Quale Press

ISBN: 978-1-935835-36-3 trade paperback edition
LCCN: 2025932458

Cover: Artwork by Max Ernst from the front cover of the 1922 Au Sans Pareil edition of *Répétitions*.

All illustrations by Max Ernst

A ClearSound book from
Quale Press

www.quale.com

CONTENTS

REPETITIONS

Misadventures of Immortals

REPETITIONS

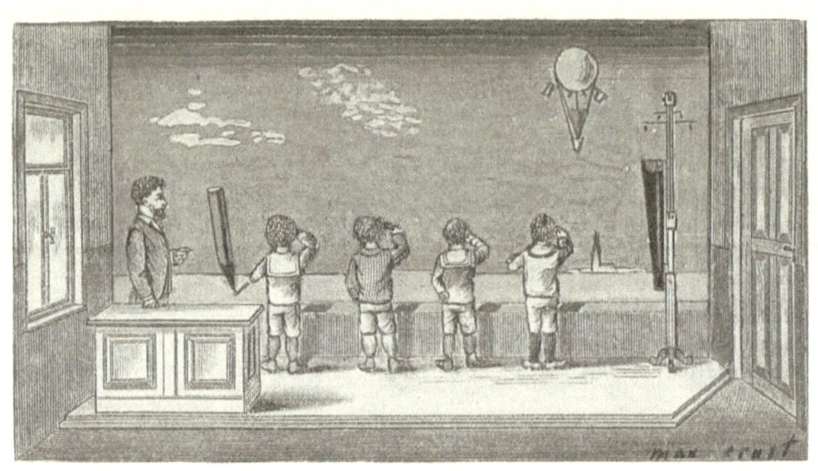
max ernst

REPETITIONS

Poems by Paul Éluard

Artwork by Max Ernst

MAX ERNST

From a corner deft incest
Spins the virginity of a petite dress
From a corner the wide-open sky
Bestows white spheres on storm's thorns.

From a corner bereft of each witnessing eye
We wait for anguish's fish.
From a corner the vehicle of summer's greenery
Majestic and eternally frozen.

From youth's radiance
Some lamps are lit far into the night
The first reveals her breasts that kill red insects.

SUITE

For the brilliance in the air of the day's delights
For thriving effortlessly on the tastes of colors
For feasting on loves' laughter
For eyes opening at the last instant

She's totally blissed out.

MANIA

After years of wisdom
Through which the world was as transparent as a needle
Are there nothing else than sweet nothings?
After having fought honored and squandered a fortune
More than a sole red lip with one red mark
And more than one white leg with its white foot
Where do we think we are?

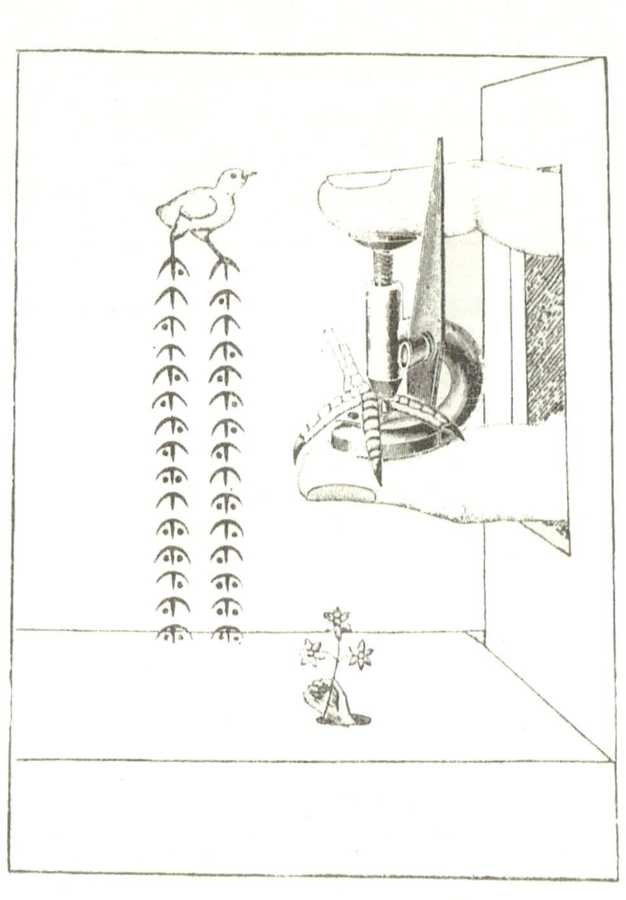

INVENTION

Legality lets sand flow.
Every transformation's possible.

Off in the distance, the sun sharpens on stones its rush to finish.
The landscape's description matters little,
Just a fulfilling stretch of harvests.

With my two eyes clear,
Like water and fire.

What role does the root play?
Despair has shattered every bond
And lifts hands to its head.
A seven, a four, a two, a one.
A hundred women in the street
That I'll never see again.

The art of loving, unconventional art, the art of dying well, the art of thinking, inchoate art, the art of smoking, the art of enjoyment, the art of the Middle Ages, decorative art, the art of reasoning, the art of reasoning well, poetic art, mechanical art, erotic art, the art of being a grandfather, the art of the dance, the art of seeing, the art of agreement, the art of caressing, Japanese art, the art of playing, the art of eating, the art of torture.

However, I have never found what I write in what I love.

NEARER TO US

Rush and rush release
And find everything pick up everything
Release and wealth
Rush so fast that the string breaks
From the cry an enormous bird makes
An always outdated flag.

OPEN DOOR

Life's so accommodating
Approach me, if I draw you close it's a game,
Angels of bouquets whose flowers alter color.

SUITE

Sleeping, moon in one eye and sun in the other,
Love in the mouth, a beautiful bird in the hair,
Adorned much like fields, woods, roads and the sea,
Beautiful and adorned throughout the world.

Scamper through the landscape,
Amid branches of smoke and all the wind's fruits,
Stone legs stuck in sand,
Caught by the waist, every muscle of the river flexed,
And the final vestiges of worry on a transmogrified face.

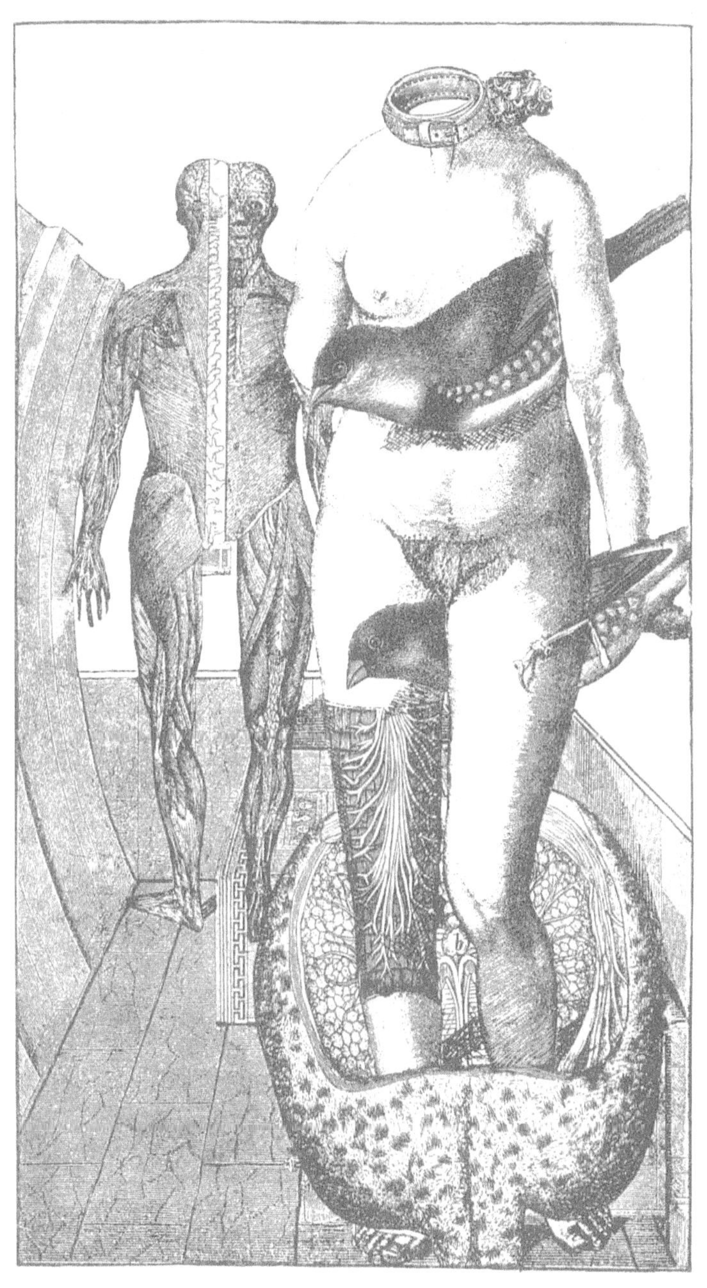

WORD

I've an easy beauty and it's blessed.
I skate across the winds' roof
I skate across the seas' roof
I've become sentimental
I no longer know who's in control
I no longer edge silk over ice
I'm noxious flowers and pebbles
I love the most convoluted clouds
I love the most naked differences among birds
I'm old but here I'm beautiful
And the shadow that trickles from the depths of windows
Spares each evening the jet black heart of my eyes.

RIVER

The river I've under my tongue,
Water you can't imagine, my tiny boat,
And, with curtains drawn, let's talk.

SHADOW WITH SIGHS

Light sleep, small propeller,
Small, warm, heart aloft.
Prestidigitator's love,
Sky laden with hands, veins flashing,

Running colorless in the street,
Hemmed by a row of cobblestones,
He sets free the last bird
From yesterday's halo –
A single snake in each well.

Much like dreaming of prying open the gates of the sea.

NUL

What was said: I crossed the street to get out of the sun. It's way too hot, even in the shade. There's the street, four floors and my sunlit window. A cap on his head, a cap in hand, he comes to shake my hand. Would you please not holler like that, that's crazy!

Invisible blind people lay out night's underclothes. Night, moon and their hearts chase each other.

In turn, a cry: "Footprint, the footprint, I no longer see the footprint. In the end, I can no longer follow you!"

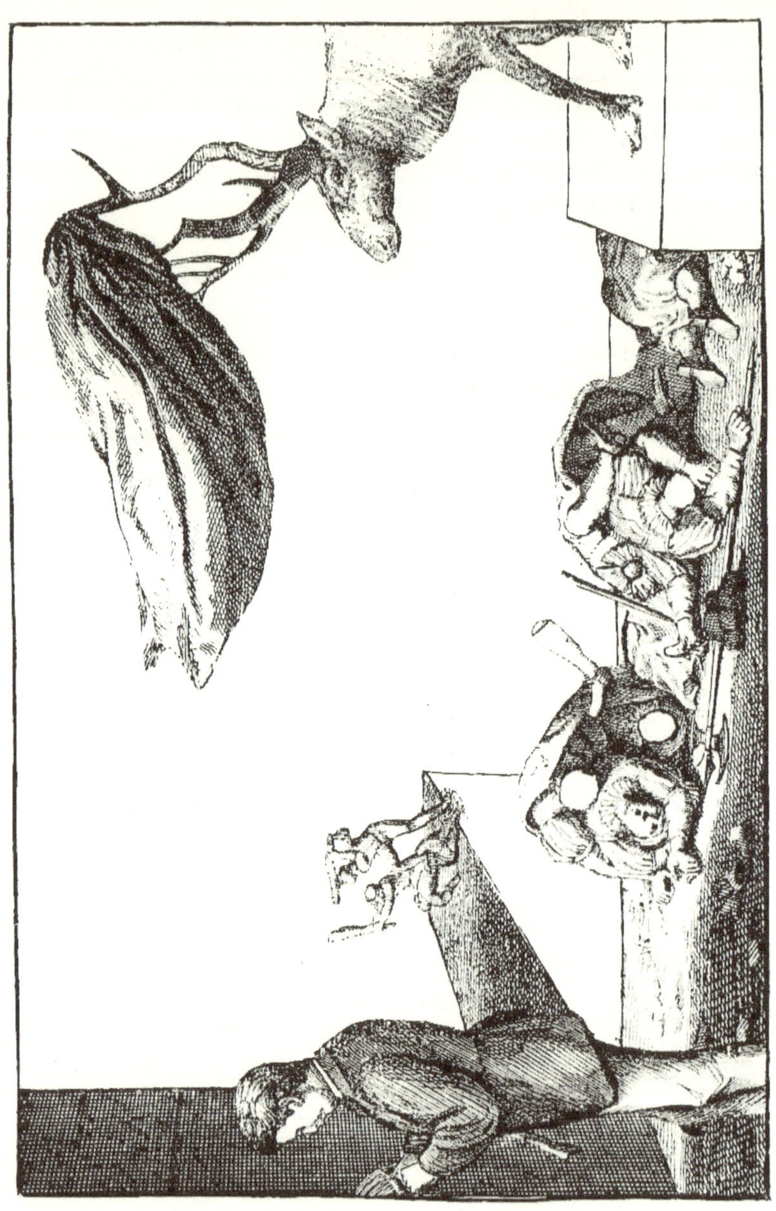

POEMS

You only had to pick a heart from a tree,
Smile and laugh, laughter and sweetness outside sensation.
Defeated, victorious and luminous, pure as an angel,
Reaching way up to the sky, amid trees.

In the distance, a beauty moans who'd rather fight
And who can't, lying at the foot of a hill.
And whether the sky's clouded or crystalline
You can't see her without loving her.

Days like fingers flexing their joints.
Flowers are dried, seeds lost,
A heat wave follows protracted white frosts.

From a poor dead man's eye. Painting porcelains.
Music, pale bare arms.
Winds and birds conjoin – the sky shifts.

ENDPOINT

Imagine heartaches carved under torn sails
Those little devotees of meandering rivers
Where one strolls to drown
We'll run about joylessly
We'll paddle
Into the neck of the waters

We'll sport a boat.

SHEEP

Night face, close your eyes
Gardens along the street, close them off
Intelligence and impudence
Restlessness and restfulness
These sad evenings at every moment
Glass and glass door
Inviting and reasonable
Sparse and laden with fruit
Flowering tree fruit tree
Scram.

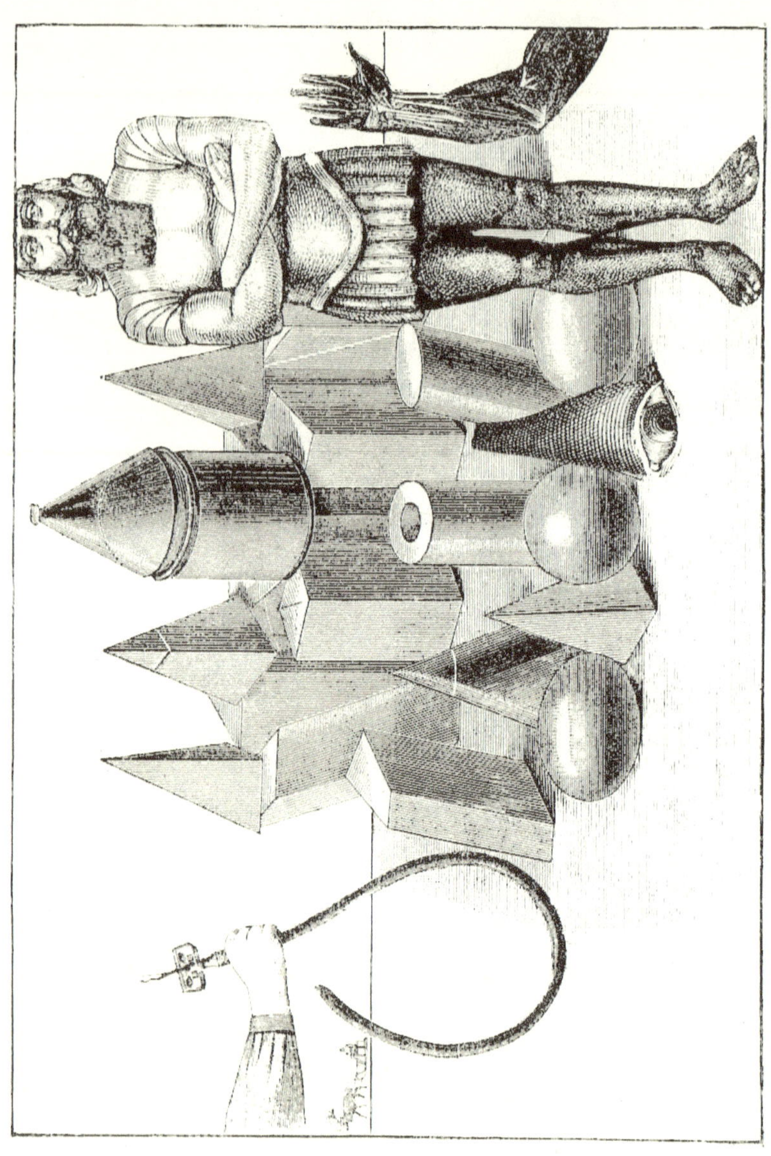

SOLE

Within her body's serenity she possessed
A runt of a snowball the color of an eye
She carried on her shoulders
A taint of silence taint of rose
Shroud her aura
Her hands and supple curves and singers
Shatter light

She sang the minutes without falling asleep.

LIFE

Smile at visitors
Who come out of hiding
When she appears she sleeps.

Every day earlier and earlier
Every season more naked
More unique

To keep pace with her gaze
She sways.

NUL

He sets a bird on the table and closes the shutters. He combs his hair, in his hands his hair's softer than a bird.

She tells the future. And I'm charged with verifying it.

Bruised heart, hurt soul, broken hands, white hair, prisoners, all the waters lay on me like an open wound.

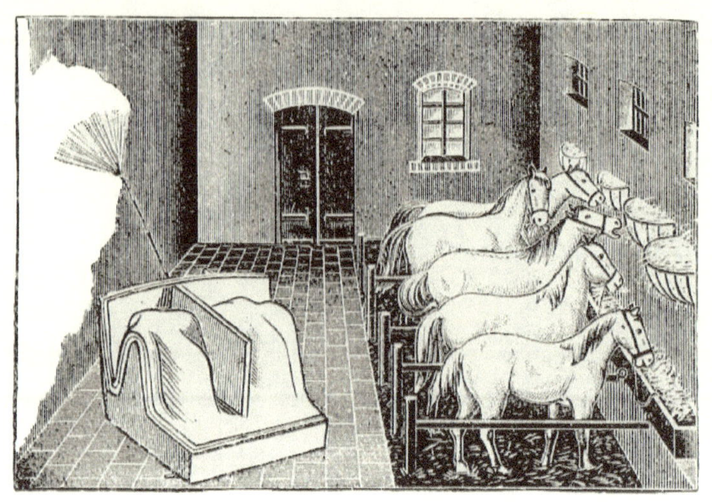

INTERIOR

In a few moments
A painter and his model
Will make their escape.

More virtues
Or fewer misadventures
I spot a statue

Some sort of almond
A laquered medallion
For the most monumental boredom.

CLOSE BY

Longest night and whitest road.
Lamps, I'm so much closer to you than the light.
Butterfly bird of habit
Broken wheel of my exhaustion
In a place in a good mood
Blank signal and signal
To the spinning clock arms.

CLOSE BY

Oscillating sun
Blank signal and signal to the clock's spin
To the unified caresses of a hand on heaven
To birds cracking open the book of the blind
And with one wing after another between this hour and another
Sketching the horizon uncurling shadows
Which narrows the world down when I squint my eyes.

IMPATIENT

So saddened by false calculations
He writes his numbers backwards
And falls asleep.

A more beautiful woman
And never before found,
Sought rosy ideas for barely fifteen years,
Laughed without knowing it, with nary a compliment
To youths' time.

For the gathering
Of what passed close by
The other day,

With the woman who was bored,
Hands on ground,
Beneath a cloud.

The lamp flared at the storm's transgressions
Without fail during August's exceptional weather,
The passionate one kissed the air, her companion's cheek,
Shut her eyes
And like evening's leaves
Fell from the horizon.

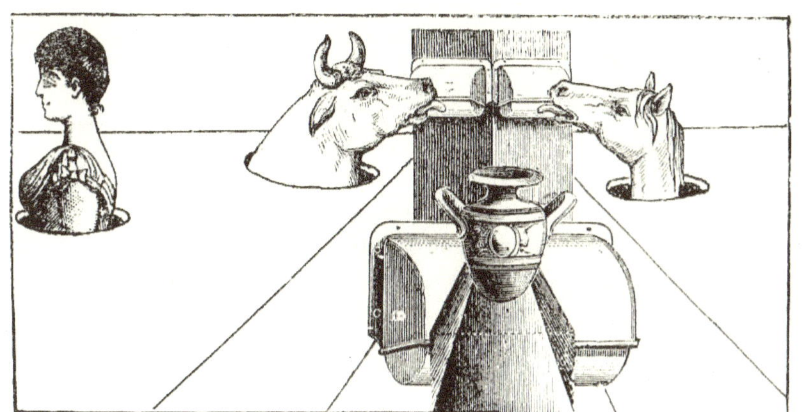

GLOW

Impeccably cultivated field,
Honeyed dawn, blossoming sun,
Runner keeping ahold of a sleeper by a thread
(Knot of understandings)
And throwing him onto his shoulders:
"He's never been newer,
He's never been heavier."
Once worn, he'll be lighter,
Useful.
Brilliant summer sun with:
Warmth, sweetness, stillness
And then, so quickly,
Those bearing flowers in the air touch earth.

LARGE UNINHABITABLE HOUSE

In the heart of a breathtaking island
That her limbs enfold
She inhabits a dazzling world.

Flesh you show to the nosy
Lingers there waiting for harvest
Roll and roll down river banks.

Biding time to see beyond
Eyes wide open within the wind of her hands
She imagines the horizon has untied its belt for her.

DEATH IN CONVERSATION

Who bears your face?
The good and the bad
Compellingly beautiful
Innumerable gymnastics
Surpassing in movements
Colors and kisses
Night's grandiose gestures.

ALL THE MORE REASON

Lights in air,
Air around a column half spent, half lit,
Let the children in,
Every greeting, every kiss, every thanks.

Around her mouth
Her laugh's invariably different,
It's a treat, it's desire, it's torture,
A madwoman, a flower, a Creole strolling by.

Nude, never the same.
I'm very ugly.
Time for kindness, snows, medicinal herbs,
Snow squalls,
Time in fixed allotments,
Statues' flowing satins.
The temple transmutes into a fountain
And hand replaces heart.

To love me you'd have to have known me back then,
So sure of the next day.

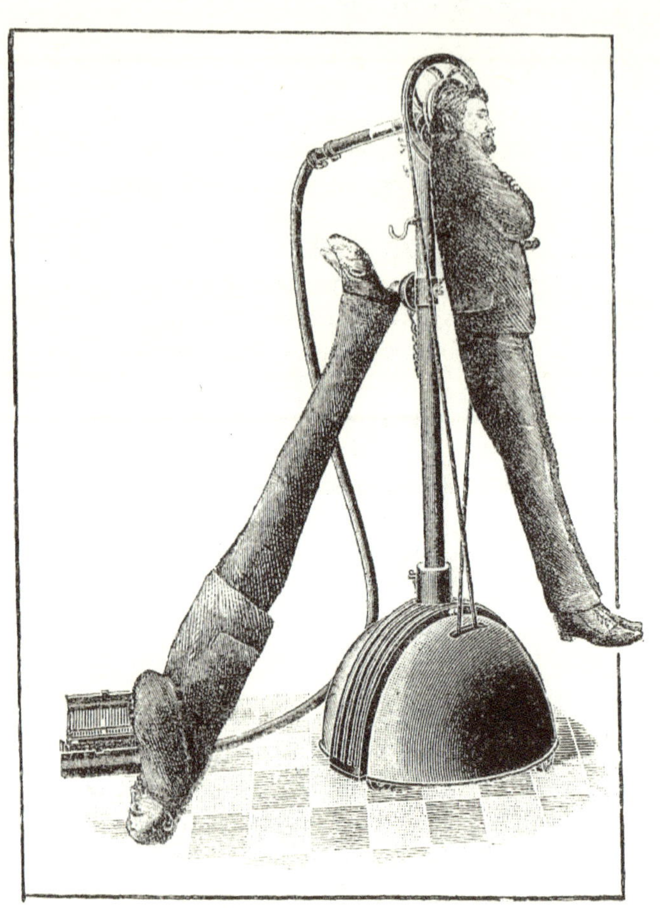

WHICH ONES?

While it's easy
And while she's smiling
Let's get dressed and undressed.

RIBBONS

Tangible alarm from which, without fail, future pain issues.

It's OK: practically imperceptible. It's a sign of superior nobility.

No surprise, a woman or a kind child of delicate linen and straw, ideas of grandeur,

Their eyes rose earlier than the sun.

The sacrificed make a gesture that articulates nothing amid the lace of every other gesture, imaginary, five or six of them, towards the resting place where no one lurks.

Notice that they've taken refuge in the bare branches of a desperate civility, of a wreath chiseled by gusts of wind.

Get a grip, ropes of life. Could you take further liberties?

Meager tools,

And hands squeezing a balloon to burst it, just like a man's blood spurting onto his face.

And wings that are attached to earth and sea.

DELIBERATELY

Blind and clumsy, ignorant and weak,
Forgetting this day,
Sketching next month,
Street corners, alleys as far as the eye can see.
Stretching out I imitate them
In my generation's deep and broad night.

TO THE MINUTE

The instrument
As you see it.
Let's hope
And
Let's hope
Farewell
Don't you dare
That eyes
As you see it
Day and night have done well.
I observe it I see it.

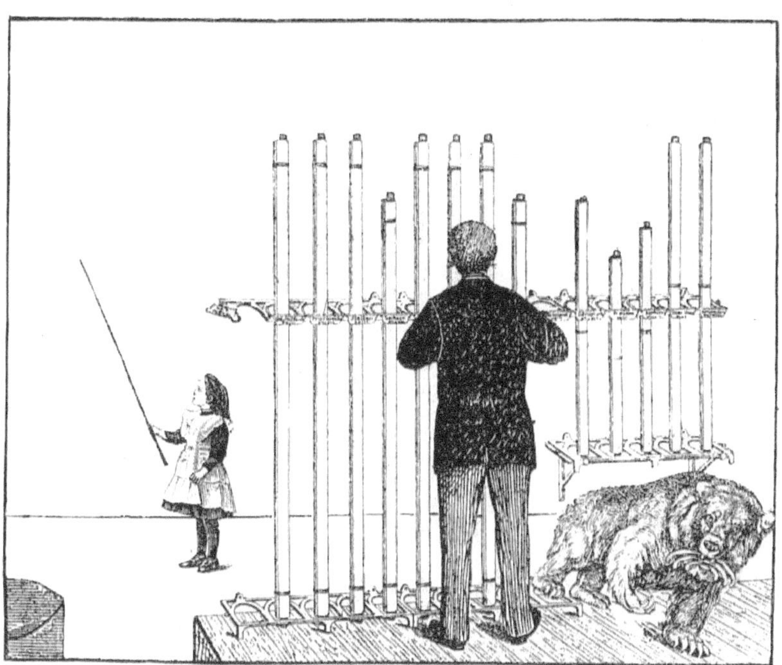

PERFECT

Miracle of fine sand
Pierces leaves flowers
Blossoms into fruit
And fills shadows.

Everything's finally distributed
Everything's misshapen and lost
Everything disintegrates and vanishes
Death without consequences.

In the end
Light's no longer natural
Voracious pulsating heat star
She abandons color
She abandons her face

Mute blind one
Everywhere she's the same and empty.

ROUND

From under a sun emerges surfaces a landscape
A woman gets all worked up
Weaves her shadow about her legs
And she alone hopes the most arcane hopes.

I find her without suspicion without doubt in love
Instead of converging paths
Of light dwindling to a point
And impossible movements
Profile's massive door
With plans debated adopted
With thoughtful emotions
Journey disguised and reconciliation arriving

Profile's massive door
Vision of precious stones
Game of weaker as stronger.

IT'S NOT POETRY THAT

With eyes such as these
How's everything the same
School of the nude.
Calmly
With a drawn visage
We took oaths
A hand brushing against fast-flowing hair
The sexy one's understudy's mouth teases and drops
And we stick out our chin that spins like a top.

DEAF EYE

Paint my portrait.
It'll be hijacked to fill in all the spaces.
Paint my portrait soundlessly, only silence
Unless – if – save – except –
I don't hear you.

It's uncertain, it's no longer uncertain.
I'd like to resemble –
Unfortunate coincidence, among other important matters.
Without being spent, head overloaded
By my hands' actions.

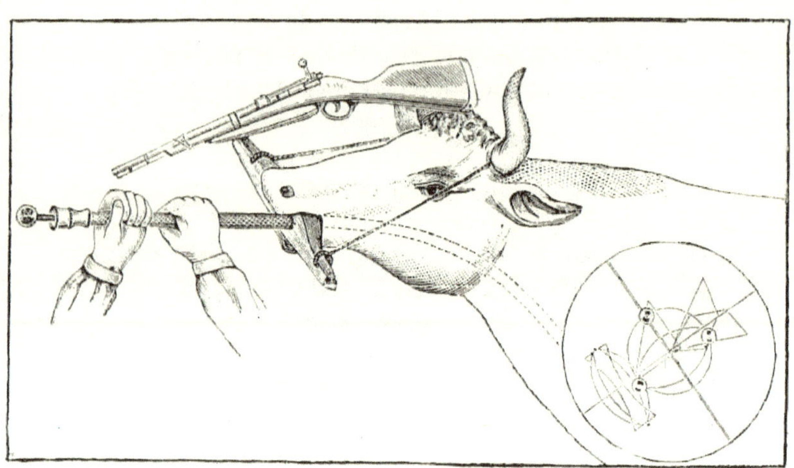

MISADVENTURES OF IMMORTALS

as revealed by

Paul Éluard & Max Ernst

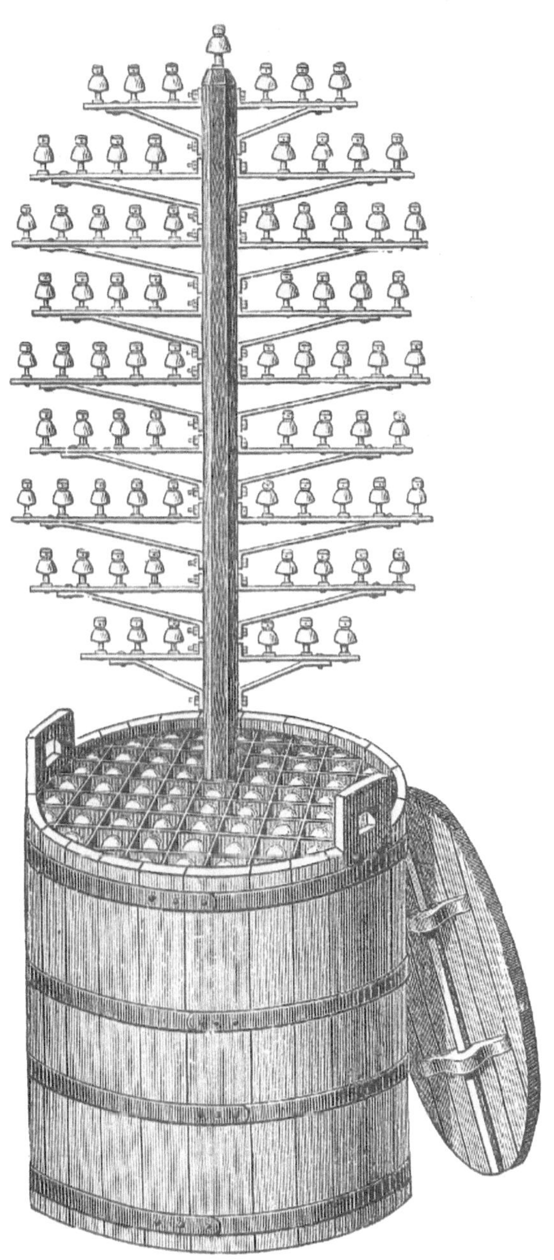

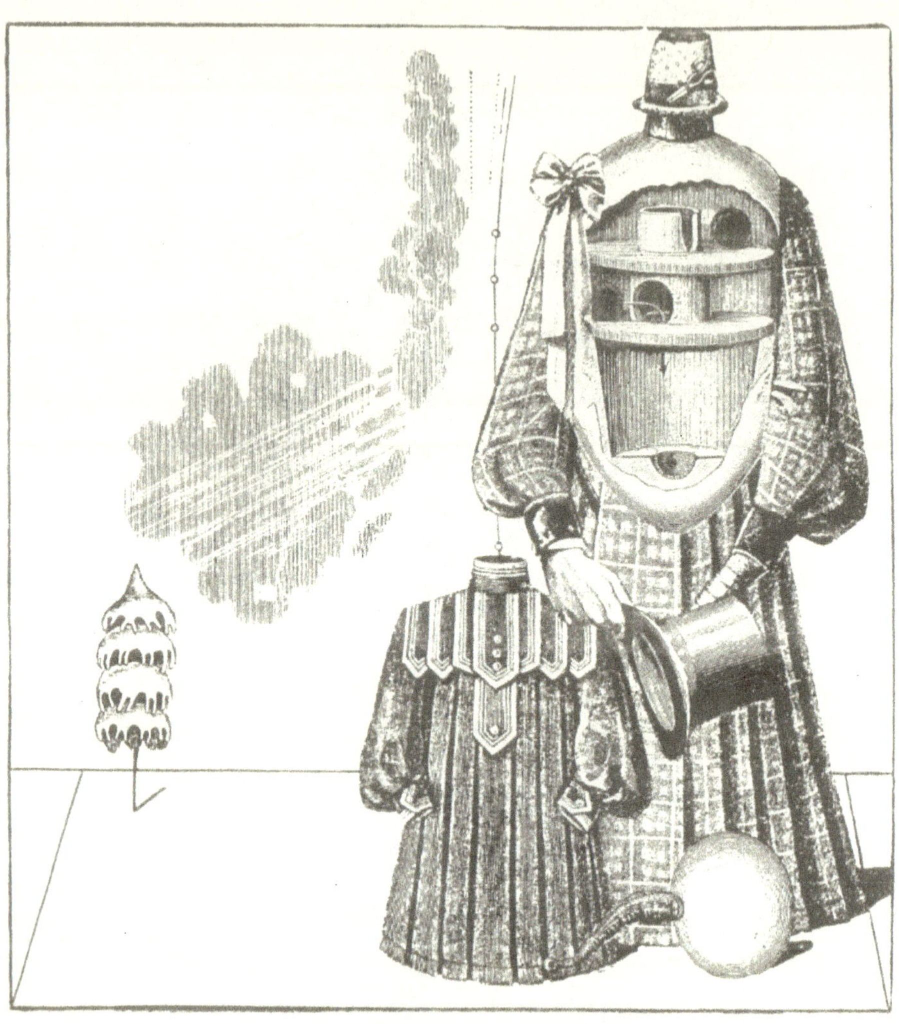

SCISSORS AND THEIR FATHER

The little one's sick, the little one's dying. He who lets us see, who trapped darkness in the pines, who dried the streets after storms. He had, he had an accommodating appetite, he carried the sweetest climate in his bones and fell in love with clock towers.

The little one's sick, the little one's dying. He now holds the world by one end and night brings him a bird by its feathers. They will throw an oversize gown on him, a gown with a typical waist, gilt edging, embroidered in a golden color, a chin strap with tassels of benevolence and confetti in his hair. The clouds decree he has only two hours left. Behind a glass pane, a needle in the air records his tremors and the divagations of his agony. In their hiding places of fine lace, pyramids curtsy to each other and dogs cower in a rebus – royalty do not like to be seen caterwauling. And the lightning rod? Where's my lord the lightning rod?

He was good. He was kind. He never stifled the wind, nor squished mud without reason. He never retreated into an oncoming flood. He's going to die. How's it nothing at all to be small?

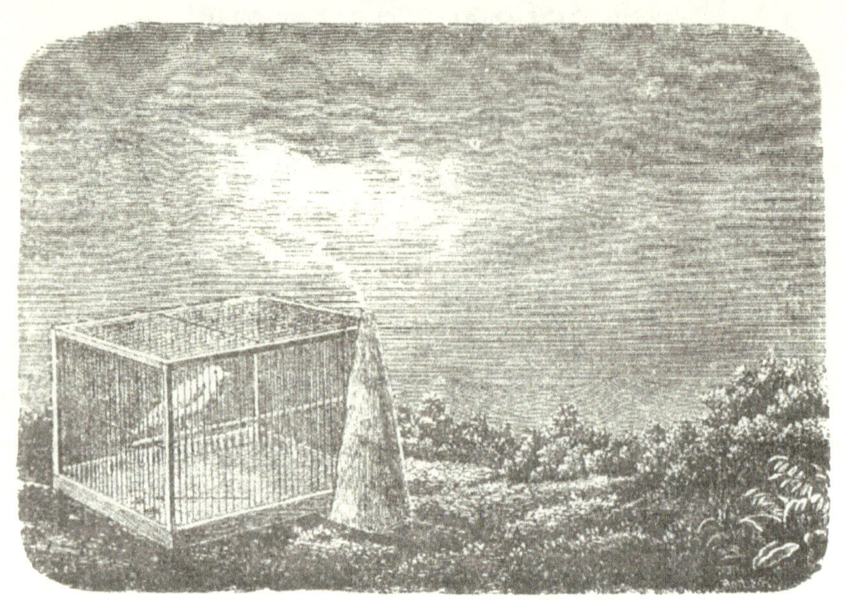

CANARY OFFICIALLY AWAKE

The canaries' dedication for study knows no bounds. The sound of footsteps doesn't shush their song, a snap of fingers doesn't prevent their prayers from becoming echoes collapsing on each other in the past. If thieves burst in, those terrible musicians unleash somewhat welcoming smiles sealed in a cage full of smoke. If it's a question of recognizing a benefactor's voice, their starving bellies have no more ears for the cannons of Mount Tabor than for the victory of Aboukir.

They don't lean out windows. At night, thunder ignites and blazes about their cage. Out in the fields, wheat stalks, obeying the law of gravity, count their grains, trees become seasoned to their leaves, the wind, with its gullet poked through with divots, pivots and falls.

Most unquestionably these canaries are masters of their own domains.

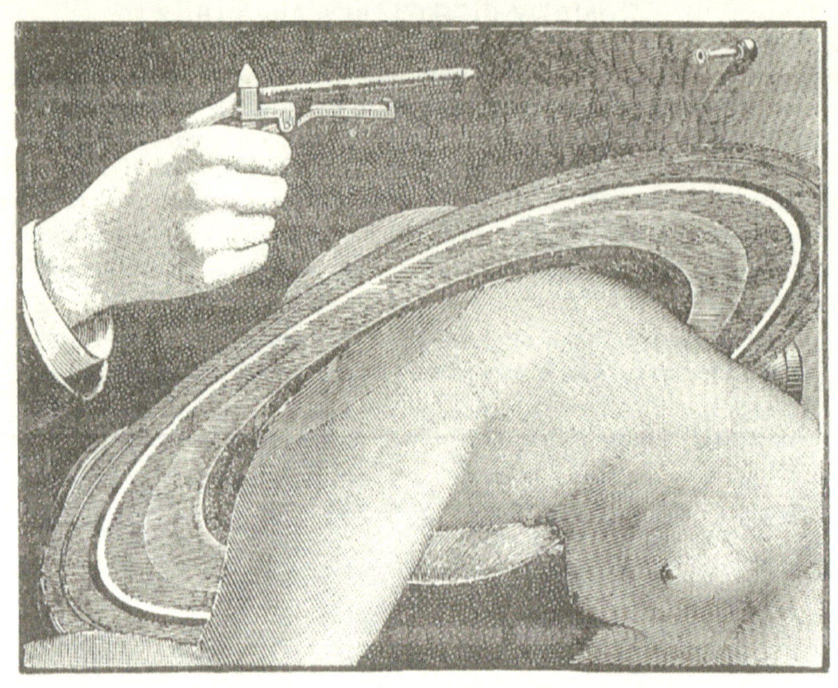

MY LITTLE MOUNT BLANC

The little black woman's freezing. Three lights still move almost imperceptibly, just as barely as the planets, despite their voyages finished, move onward as if gliding: no more wind for three hours, for three hours gravity has ceased to exist. In peat bogs, dark grasses are menaced by a magician and populate the ground along with bald men and the sweetness of their flesh that day scarcely starts to embroider with bitter clouds.

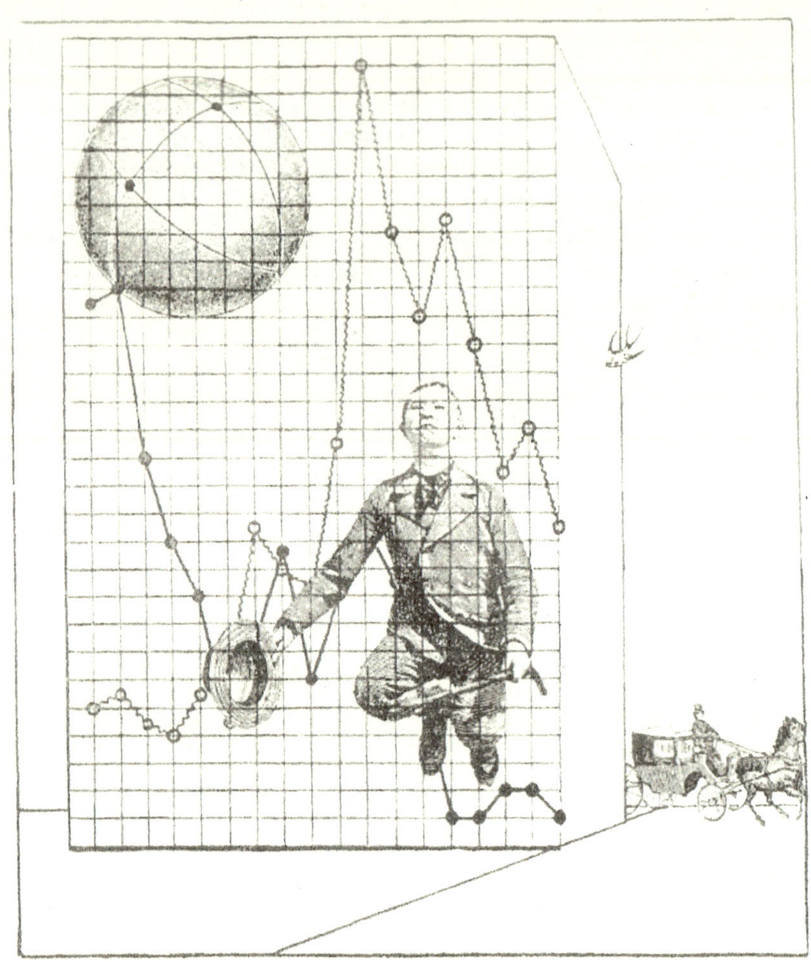

CONDEMNED BLIND MAN TURNS HIS BACK ON PASSERS-BY

A fly perched on his hand. The sun, to prevent it from flying away, sows needles around it. The sun attracts swallows afflicted with those horrible skin diseases that disfigure brutal weather. They surface from the water to walk the fields. The river isn't swarming and they've had more than enough time to arrive. But they must pack up and find all the forgotten crosses.

His feet emit the stink of lizards. He'll therefore make an auspicious marriage, a marriage with the best intentions.

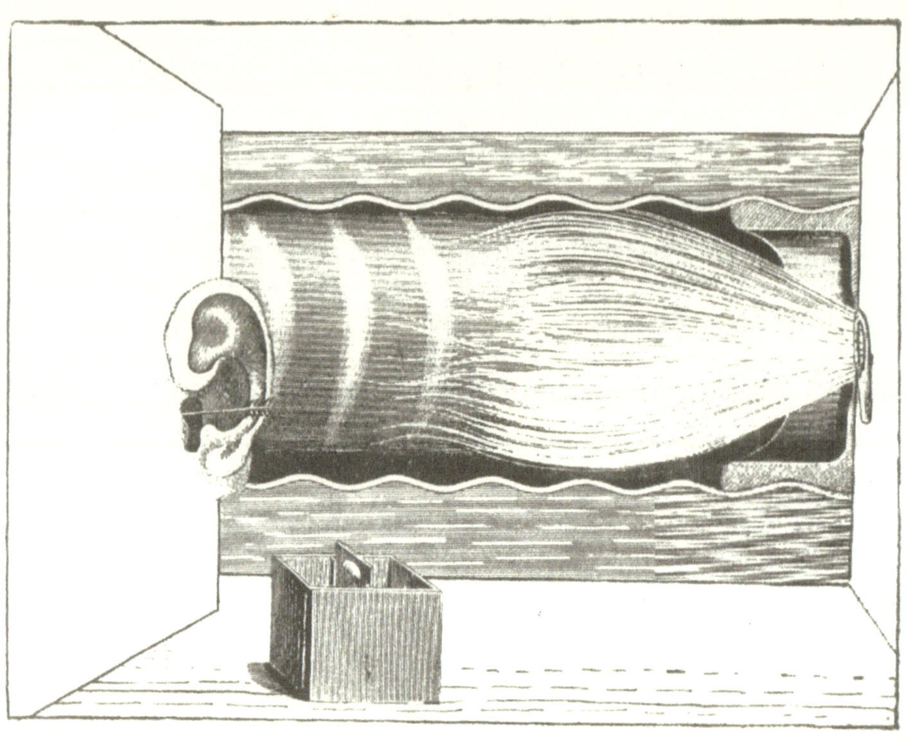

SPOTLESS WINDOWS DON'T NECESSARILY MEAN AN IMMACULATE LOVE

A priest with nondescript looks has relegated his young and pretty wife, who has demonstrated bonafide common sense, to an out-of-the-way location in order to sidestep the endless discussions that were dragging their regular sexual relations down to a halt. Cloistered in the lilacs, the heroine's father knocks up the childish joys of the unrepentant little maid.

From afar, you can hear the singing of the praises of the prisoner overlain with tiles who stands vigil before her curiously flawless keepsakes.

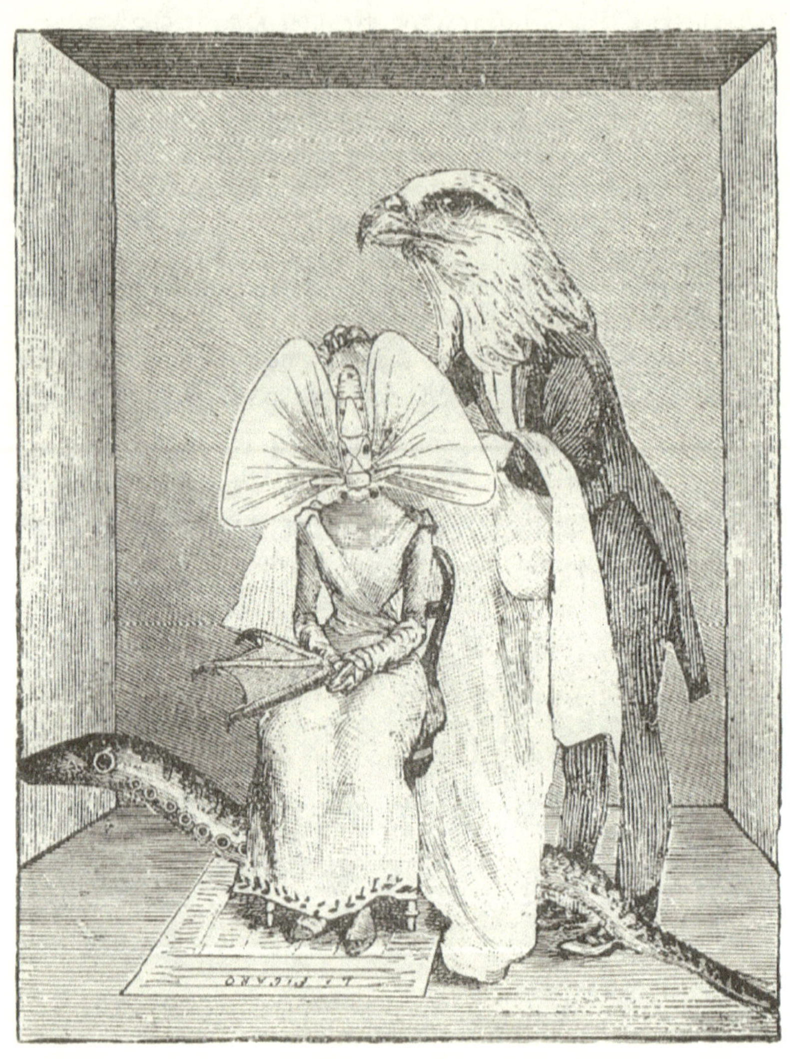

TWO SMILES MEETING

In the kingdom of hairdressers, happy folk don't waste all their time married. Apart from coquetry at pedestal tables, ducks' feet abbreviate their calls to pasty ladies. From a violin case you'll dislodge cricket chirps. In a penguin's case you'll locate a potion that'll get you killed. You'll be astonished to spot the magificence of your mirrors in eagles' talons. Take a gander at these little besainted snakes who, on the eve of their first dance, dispense sperm from their breasts. Wealth has so frustrated their ambitions that they pose an unending string of riddles to antique dealers who wander by. Heed well the sighs of those women with butterfly hairdos.

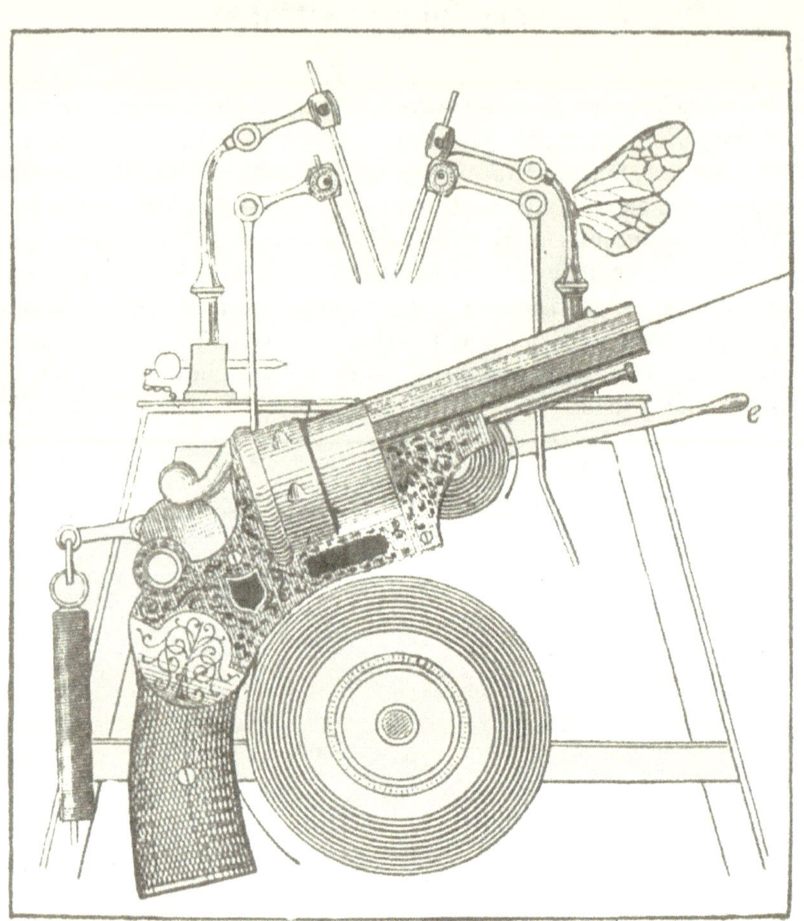
e

MELLIFLUOUS ARMFUL OF KINDLING

The spark that attracts mosquitoes to sports no longer decorates the buttonholes of farmers in the Alps and Caucasus. Threads of a bulky multi-colored spool slowed down ball movement and blocked the goal. Thankfully, since the shininess of their firearms made the duelists lower their gaze. The bystanders' derision intoxicated them with modesty. But, then, you can't be drunk all your life.

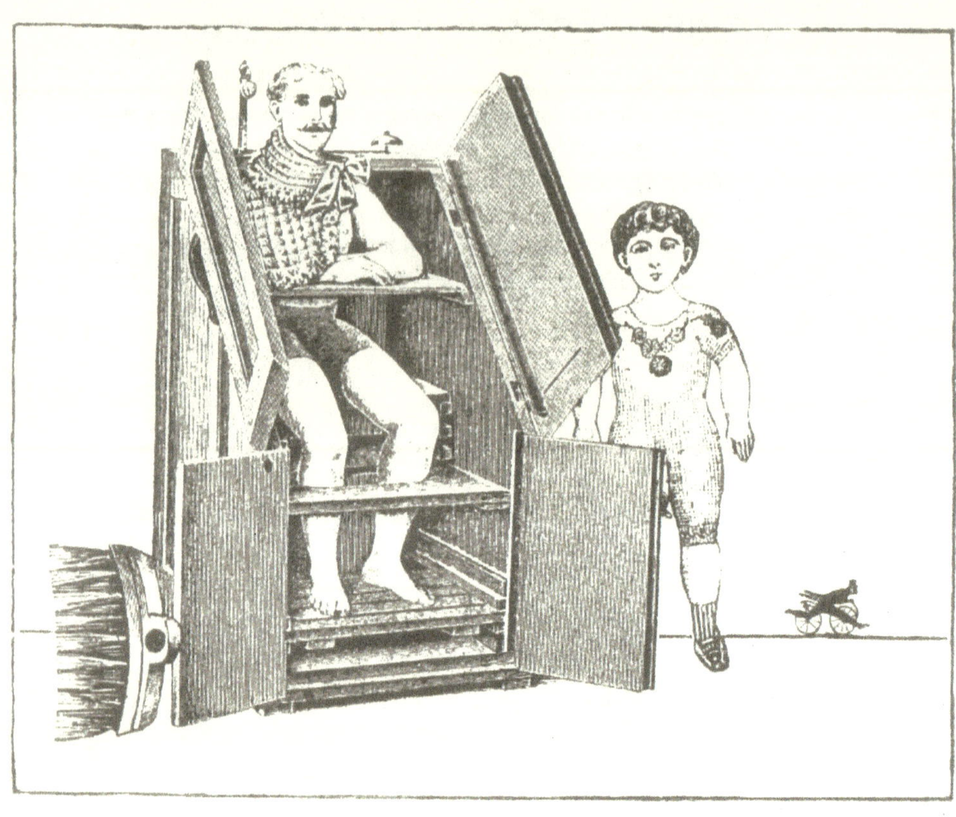

BOTH TOGETHER

Through the paper cold, schoolchildren in the void blush behind windows. A large curtain across the façade swells with little monsters.

The cabinetmaker is portrayed on his knees. Ensconced in his prototype until summer, he lovingly lets go of his sleeping son and his gold-trimmed eyes. If you impose on his shoulders the vile army of dead skittles, fish dart about stringing their wet beards from the sea's ceiling.

The fatuousness of his gestures grants him every sort of illusion. Stripped of his blue glass clothes and his unbreakable moustaches, a semi-scrupulousness prevents him from sleeping under a snow that has just started to gently fall.

His love seen from below with the benefit of perspective, he departs on the morrow.

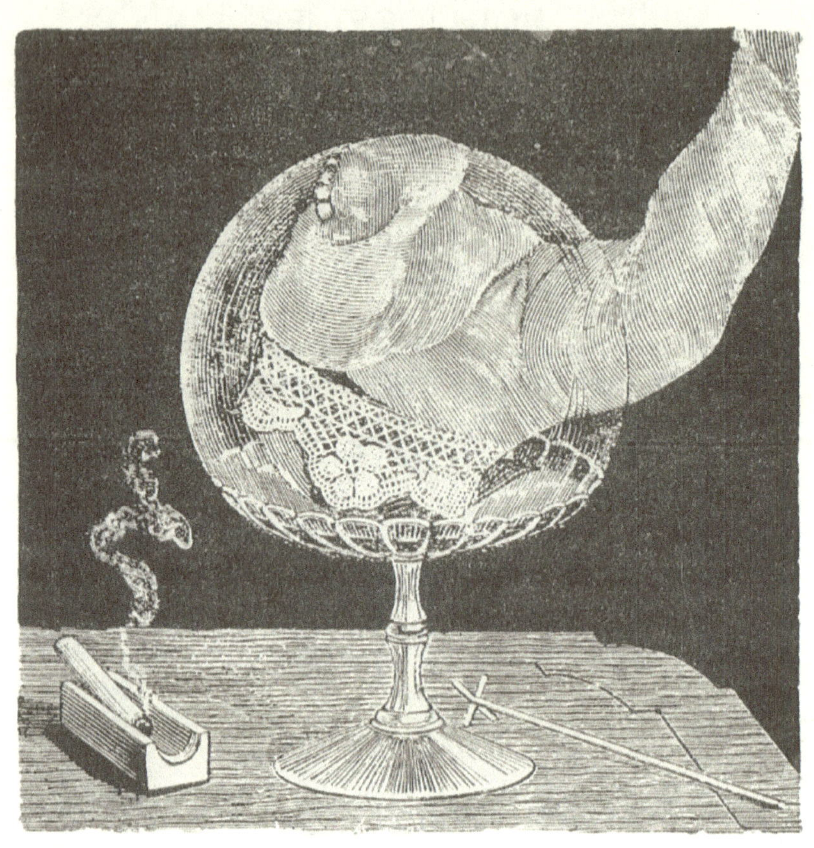

PURSUIT OF INNOCENCE

In the mountains' pellucid atmosphere one star out of ten can be seen through. Because Eskimos don't succeed in entombing light in their abominable glaciers.

In a moment of forgetfulness, light reverses direction and plants ever-so-carefully the tender kisses of a model mother. Turtledoves take advantage to cram the moon and its pain into dainty shrubbery.

Silent, our dear angel suffers the prudence of toothless sentences. First dawn, melts very quietly.

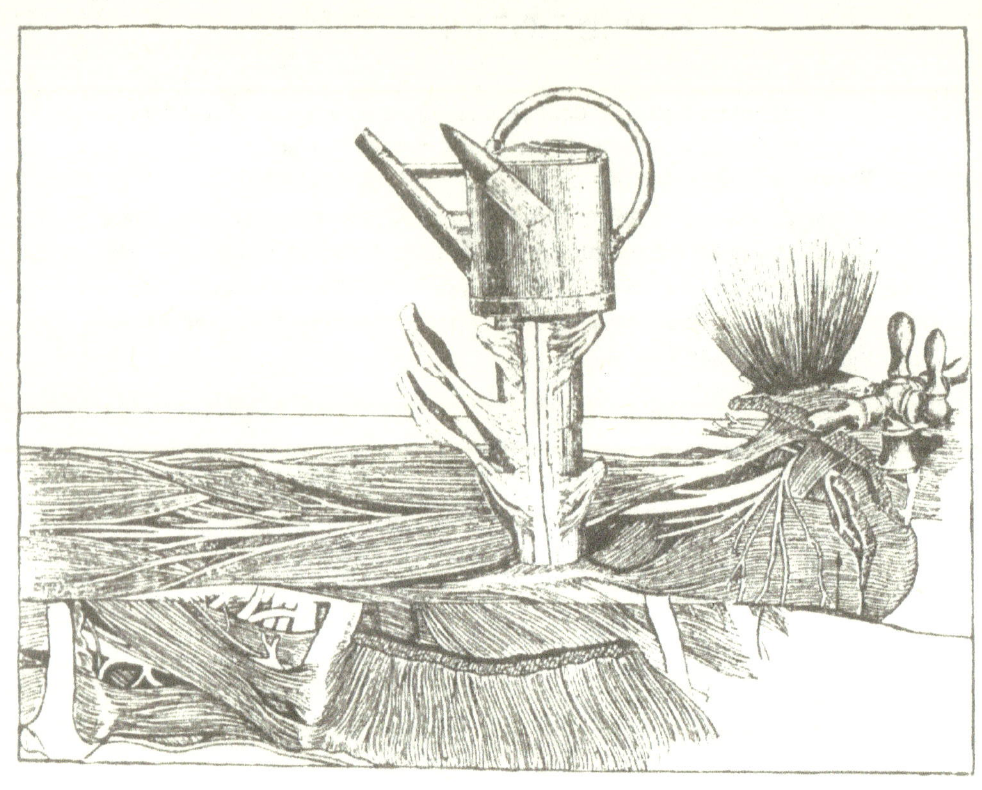

QUIET TIME

Near the lip as detected through water, the stiff-haired coquette parades her lamp in her deep rich eyes like a lover. She likes to flaunt her talent for smiling against a lustrous surface. She stretches her fingers her Amazon skin with the full force of her arm strength. She skims the tips of her breasts against the foot of the ruins and drifts into sleep at twilight with climbing plants nibbling her nails.

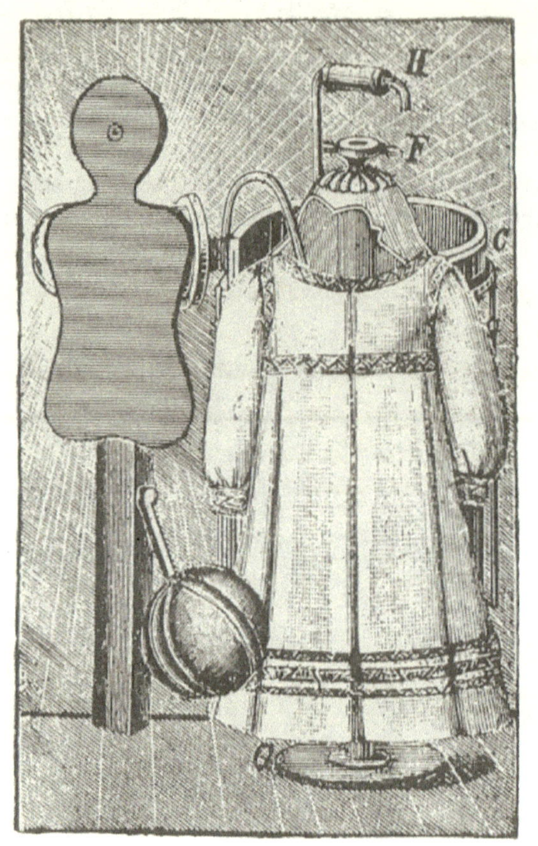
H
F
C

A FRIEND'S ADVICE

Gather freckles and beauty spots under the oaks,
track flocks of eclipse days in a boat,
ponder with pebbles in your eyes the immobility of omnipotent mannequins,
while dancing sunder the cracking of whips,
regard women, at forty, they drop their hearts into alms boxes for the poor and substitute vegetables for classic attitudes.

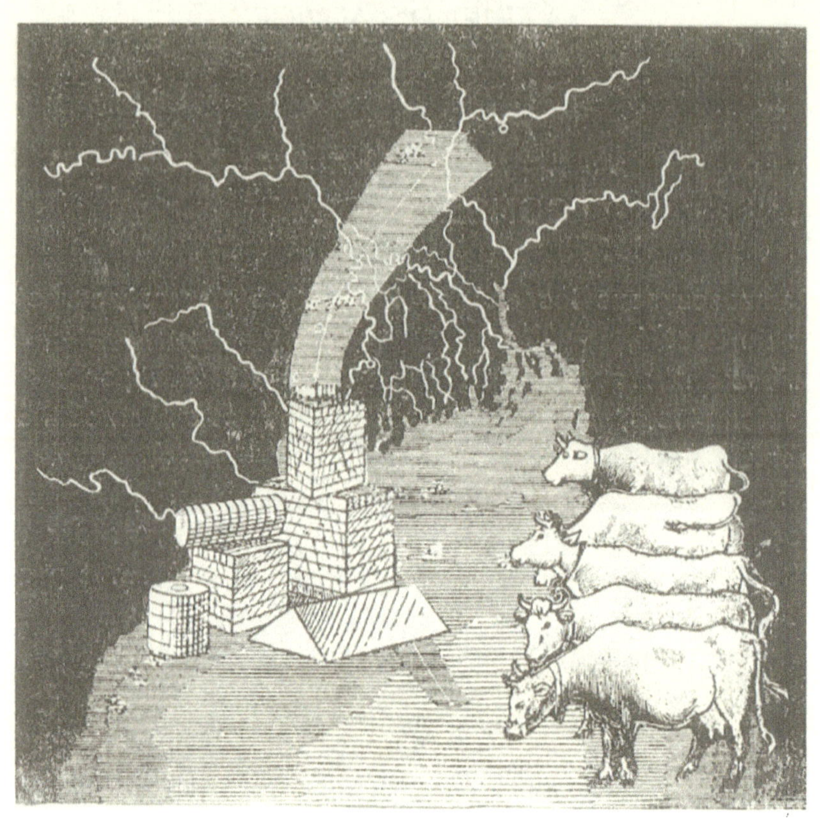

MODESTY ON PARADE

Two old men reconnect with their hearts, in their snug hammock hanging by the desert and its marvellous distractions.

Two old men with little angel hair, one in a white shirt with flapping tails, he's the one sleeping, his head resting on the other's leg.

The other, naked and his feet in the air, all red, a procuror of colors, smiles despite his indelicate pose. Nocturnal differences quickly made him shut his eyes. Yet he ever-so-tenderly tickles the stamens of the harp inched across the lioness's forehead. The mother bird's threats no longer spook him, but he needn't move his hand too much to touch the rain.

That these inseparable buddies linger in this lonely place has sufficiently fascinated a turkey, a turkey and three geese who bounded out of a bush, emerged from a pond, fled from autumn's collapse. Their curiosity has been piqued and they gingerly encircle those perverts whose vaporous testicles undulate.

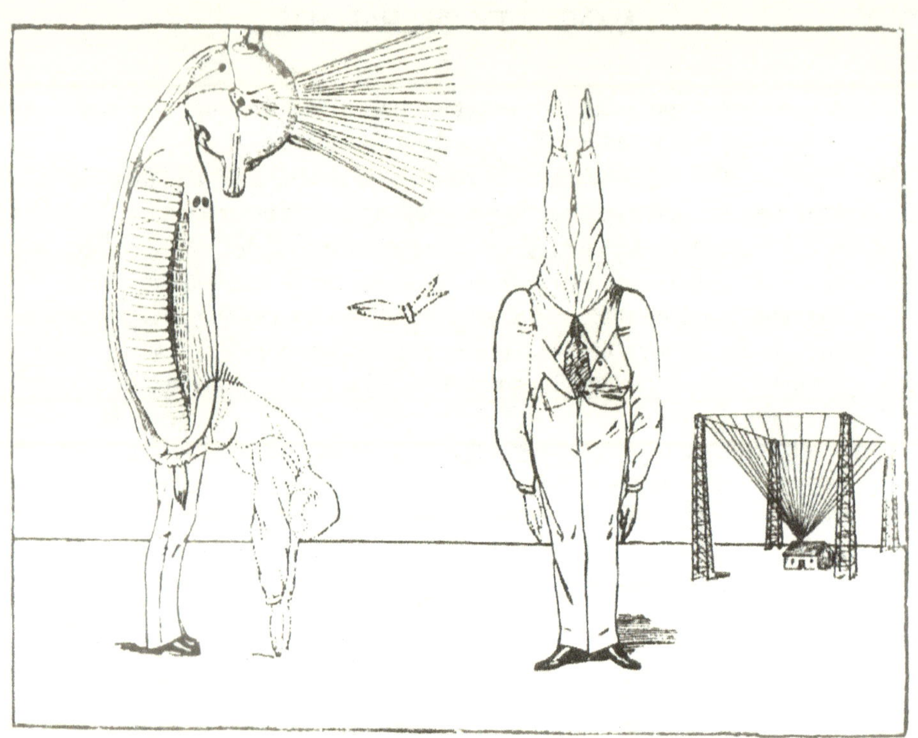

TRAVELERS' ARRIVAL

At the first sign they ran away. Their excitement scattered little varnished flags over the summit crags. Only one, indifferent . . .

By a miracle, the strongest had become powerless. He mechanically wound strips from his fingers around wings of distressed towers, swore to keep quiet, savored the tumult of children's raised voices, his hunger, his thirst and his riches. Come spring, he cultivated his garden, hand armed with a vase . . .

In the asylum, the wailing old men hugged their fellow captives, their lecherous brethren. The house was chock full of sand, windows broken and the shutters must have been shut.

We still wonder who instructed them to stop worrying about all the rest.

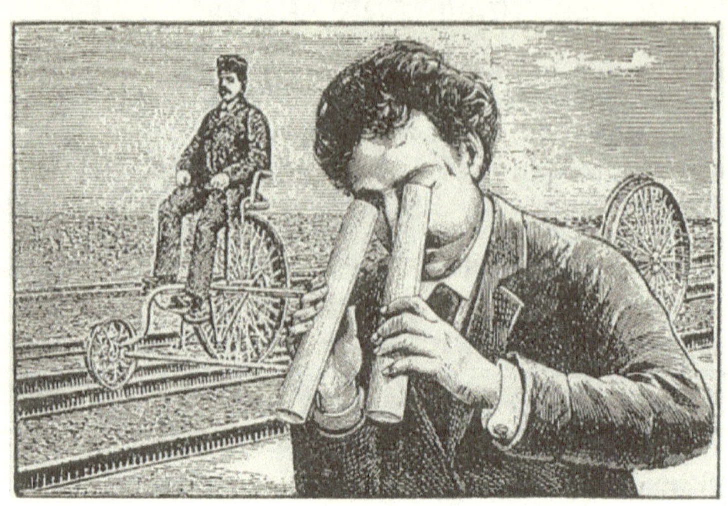

FORGOTTEN PLEASURES

At the end of the jetty, thrown from the sea, freed from prison, returned from the Indies with the assurance of huge ungovernable machines, Robert granted his curiosity license to select his route with a pin. Greasy pimples erupt and pop from his eyelids. Pain returns with the heat and despite the pain, you've got to admire his fearless soul, the surprising courage of this misbeggotten man, you can enjoy a certain little melancholy dance, out of place in this situation: the urge to sleep, which strokes his hair.

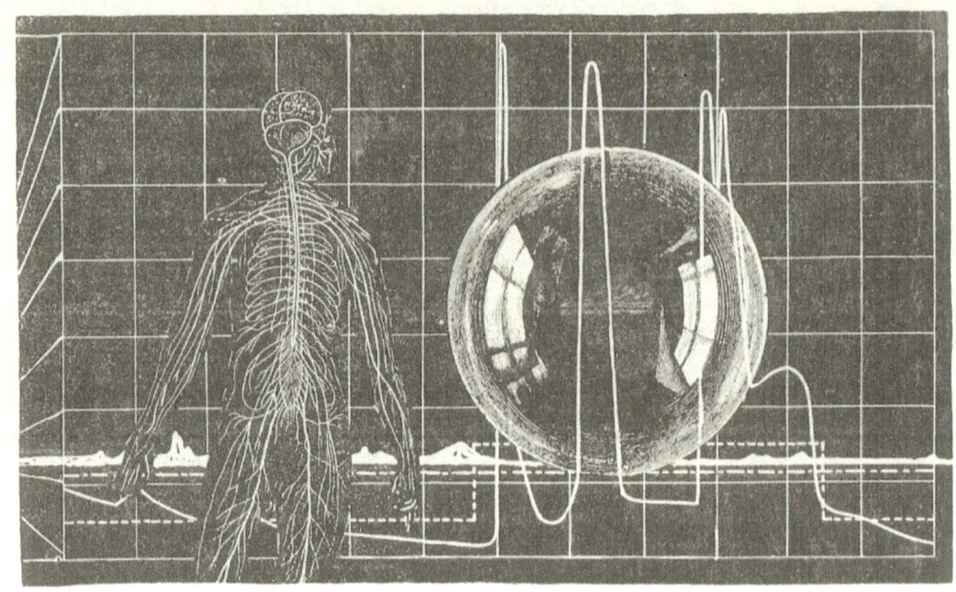

BETWEEN TWO POLES OF POLITESSE

This aerialist, soaked to the bone, produces such sensitive words for you from his goiter, beware, this aerialist epitomizes the word: sensitive. The sweet clear tone of childhood has evaporated. The precious nudity of branches releases the whiff of sanctity from where the mountain towers above everything. It has taken refuge in the globe that announces fever's fluctuations, within soap bubbles drunkards hold in their hands to ward away glow-worms, to weed peas, to avoid rampaging bulls.

This whiff of sanctity maintains an ignorance of saints Peter and Paul who have returned to see what's going on in the world. Alas! the taste for commerce has overtaken even the broad flat headlands and no one remembers the seeds of flying hats in the dead of winter.

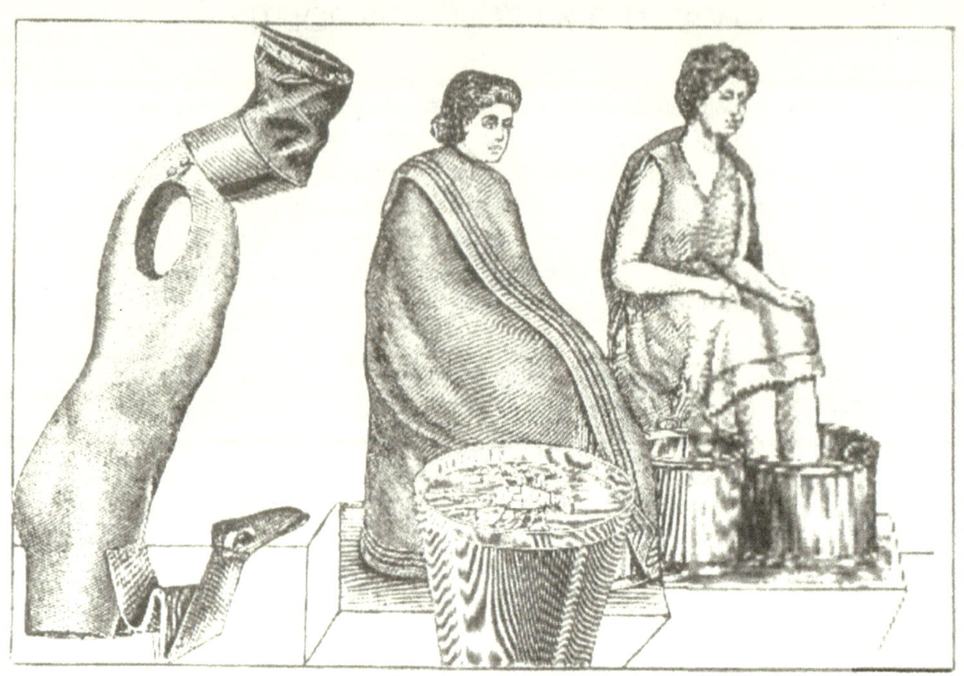

STARK NAKED IN THE STREET

Presently there are hearts, everything can be transformed into a dreidel derby. Even the white swells of long baptismal garments with which we adorn our peacocks have become electric. Our children are born naked and tanned by the sun, our children are gloved in black and capped with whimples. Our lovers divulge all their troubles. It's a fortuitous sign that they swallow their saliva and make themselves at home awaiting the deluge with their leader by the seaside. We scorn their vaingloriousness and the purity of their beliefs. Black women are lightly daubed in blue, we thin leaves from their palms, we organize them by age. Our dogs kick them but no one can prevent grass from growing under our arms. Truth: here lie hearts.

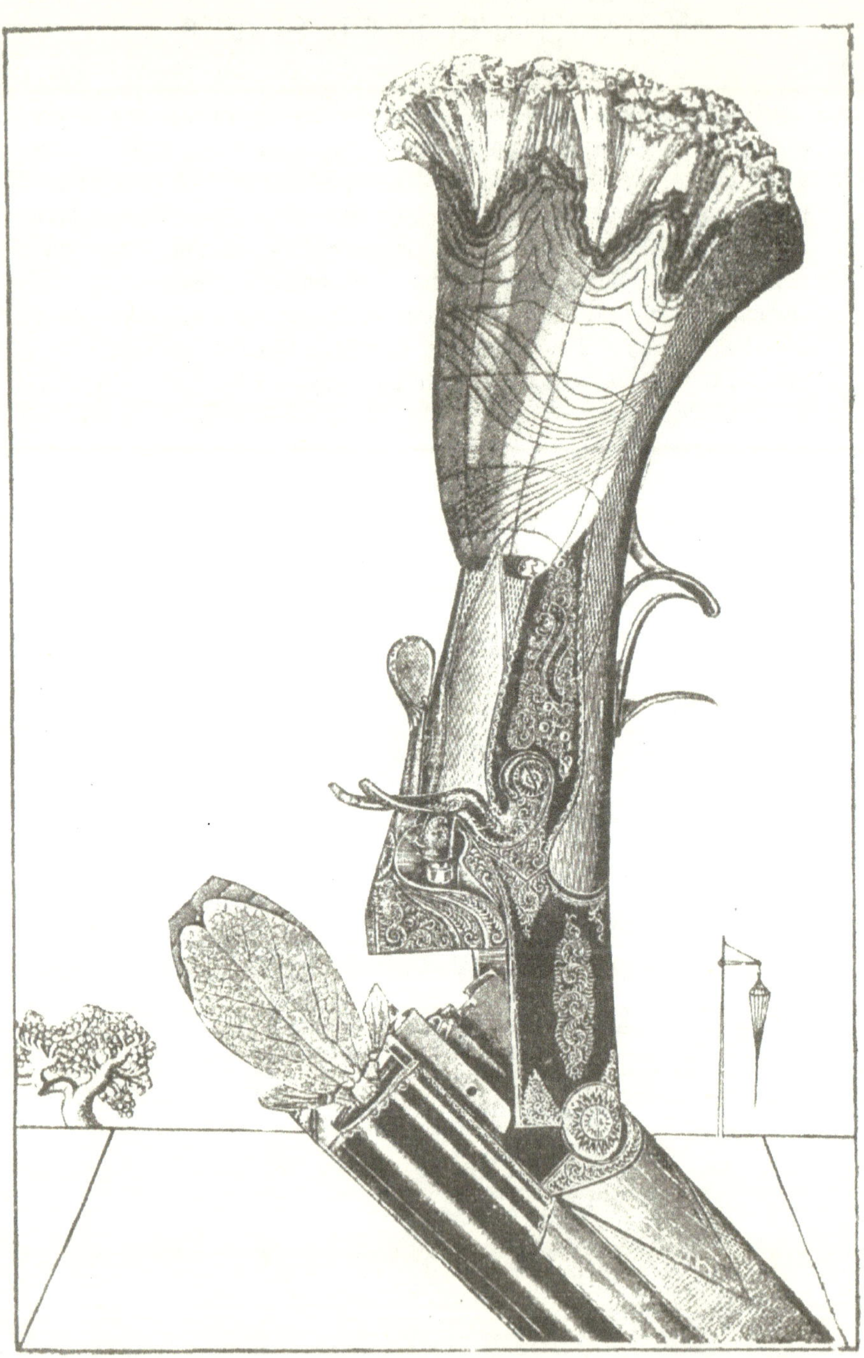

PLEASANTNESS AND USEFULNESS

No one knows teeth's tragic origins. Once upon a time, the equator frittered away the fear of heat.

Apart from despoiling our crops, she morphs harsh and physical education into honey.

The racket of hometown bells unnerves him pains him and forces his first child to jump from his mouth as wide as an amphitheater. What would you make of her, without a horizon of balloons and stunned beasts? A nameless sky, shaped by hand, made itself known and presents us with the crone wolf who, after having loved and fought all her life, wants to continue to abide under favorable terms.

When she dies, I'll be just six years old.

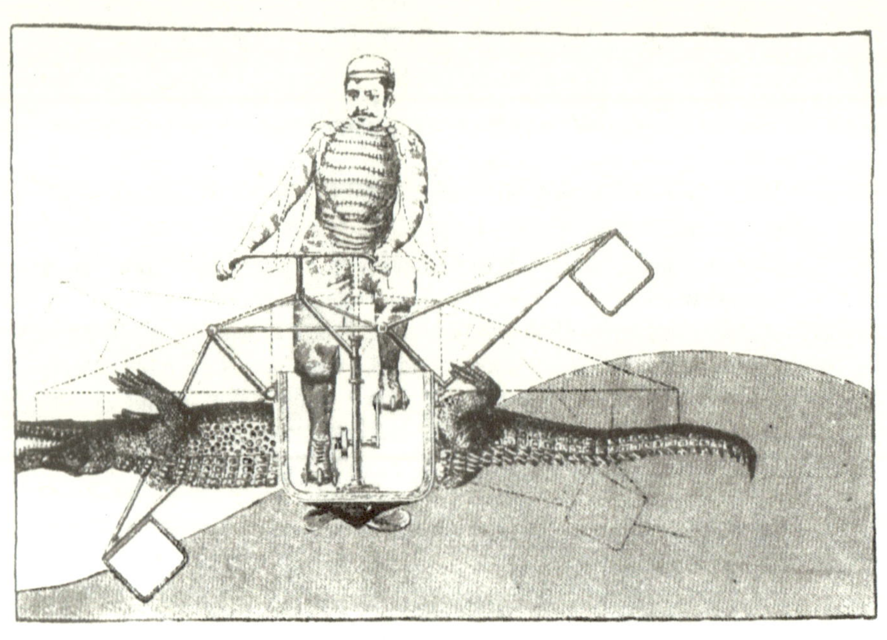

BROKEN FANS

Today's crocodiles are no longer crocodiles. Where are the good old pioneers who hung miniature bicycles and pretty icicles from your nostrils? Matching the speed of your fingers, runners at the four cardinal points were praising each other. What a treat it was then to lean with graceful nonchalance against these pleasant rivers sprinkled with pigeons and pepper!

There are no more true birds. Wires stretched across return paths in the evening did not cause anyone to trip, but, at each fake impediment, smiles overwhelmed just a smidgen more the eyes of the tightrope walkers. Dust had the smell of lightning. Once, good old fish wore cute red shoes on their fins.

There are no more authentic waterbikes, no microscopy, no bacteriology. Today's crocodiles are no longer crocodiles. Word.

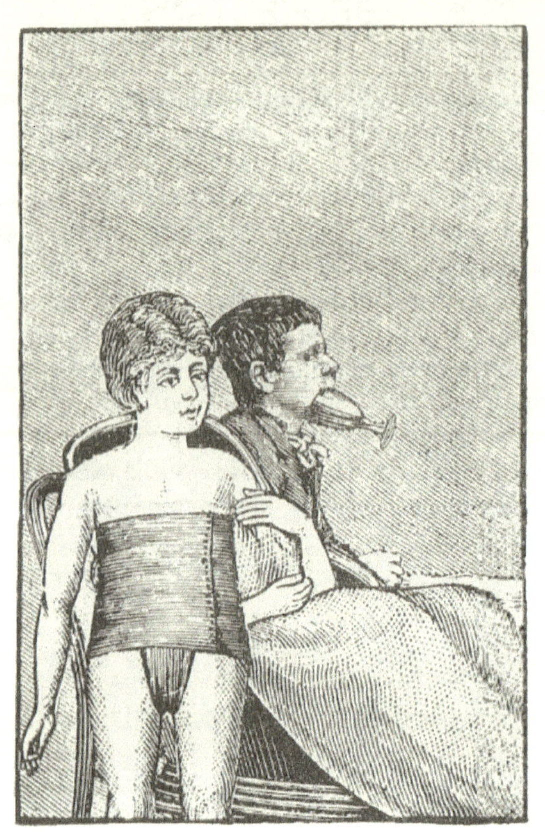

PEACE IN THE COUNTRYSIDE

In the evening, when chance lets girls' hands cup when fire consumes all the vines of the Old Continent and city stones fill all the cellars, wax and metal dancers materialize through the indifference of the feeble who patiently grind away any corporeal relief. Their companions listen, happy as can be, to their incessant, tiresome song and their children with nary a hair out of place frolic amid the debris of the final sermons.

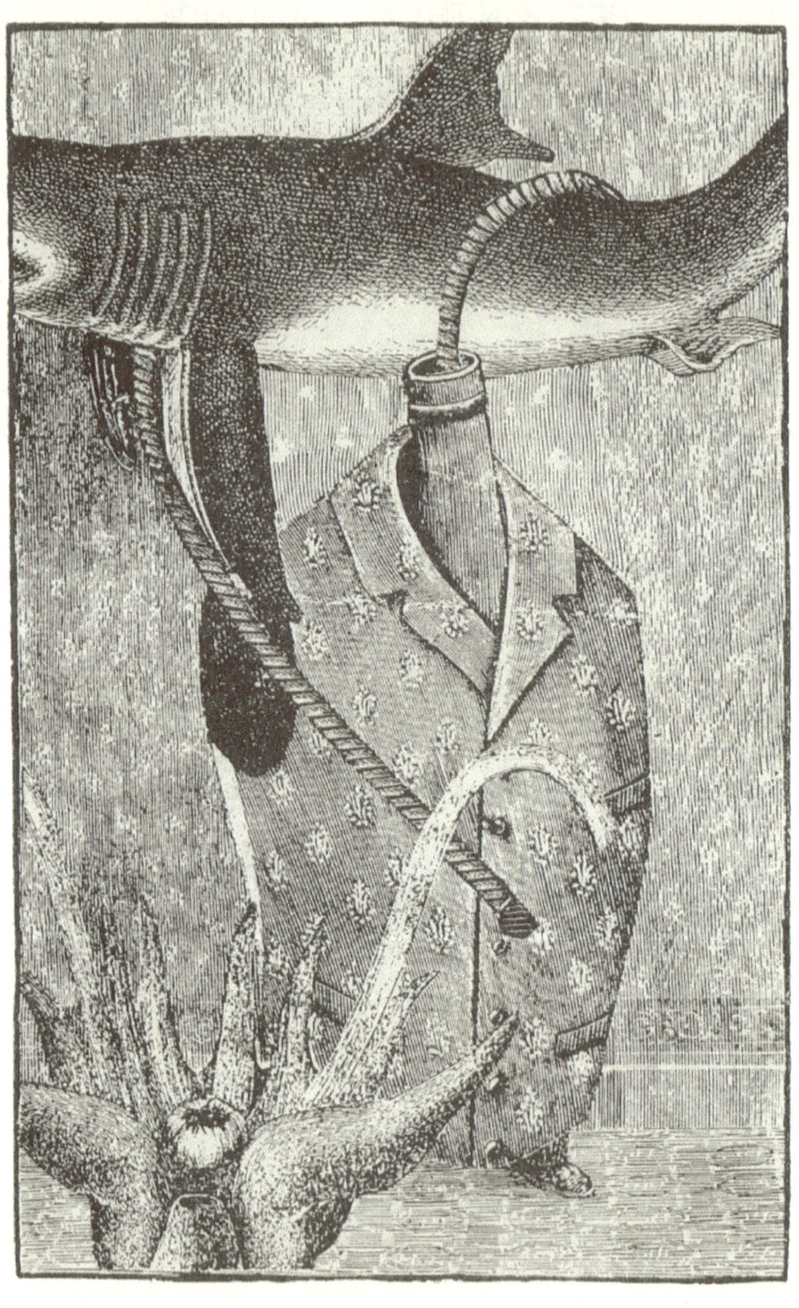

FUGITIVE

He elected to drown himself rather than enlist. They all abandoned it – their security, their past, their happiness, hope. The rope he carries does not match the usual towropes. Her chest will serve as his pillow, the extreme sweetness of her unrestraint will awaken him. The peacefulness he accumulates is stripped of a thousand fibers of burnt muslin and the floating leaves of a clinging plant. Hails from the ships make her natural decorations blossom into future arrangements.

Always points of view and the least means.

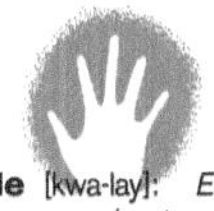

quale [kwa-lay]: *Eng.* n. 1. A property (such as hardness) considered apart from things that have that property. 2. A property that is experienced as distinct from any source it may have in a physical object. *Ital.* pron.a. 1. Which, what. 2. Who. 3. Some. 4. As, just as.

www.ingramcontent.com/pod-product-compliance
Lightning Source LLC
LaVergne TN
LVHW050953080826
845145LV00005B/1491

9781935835363